DRE

WHAT **YOU** CAN DO T... ...OTE

BIG

YOUR **BUSINESS** AT A **LOW COST**

DREAMS

WRITTEN BY

INTERNATIONAL **SEO EXPERT**

RICKY WHITING

Dream BIG Dreams

What You Can Do to Promote Your Business at a Low Cost

By Ricky Whiting

Get More Customers & Sales with These Proven Tips

Prologue

If you're looking to promote your business on a budget, this is the book for you. This guide provides all the information you need to market your business using SEO, social media, email, and more. With this advice, you can see a difference in your traffic and sales within just 30 days.

To learn more about how you can market your business on a budget, please sit back and enjoy this book.

When I was starting my business, I was looking for ways to promote it cheaply. I found that using all methods of marketing- from SEO to social media to email marketing- worked best.

I was able to see a difference in the amount of traffic to my website and the number of customers and sales my business generated.

If you're starting a new website, existing website, or e-commerce website, I highly recommend using these tips and strategies to see success in the next 30 days.

Shocking fact: up to 80% of potential customers could be lost to businesses without a website

There is no one-size-fits-all approach to marketing your business. What works for one company may not work for another.

However, there are a number of low-cost methods you can use to promote your business. Here are a few tips:

1. Use SEO to improve your search ranking.
2. Utilise social media networks to build brand awareness.
3. Send out email newsletters to keep customers updated on new products and promotions.
4. Generate traffic through outbound marketing efforts such as online ads and PR campaigns.
5. Track your results and optimise your campaigns based on the data collected.
6. Rinse and repeat!

By following these tips, you can see a significant difference in the amount of traffic to your website and the number of customers and sales your business generates.

Implement these strategies now to see success in the next 30 days. Good luck!`

This Book Is For You...

This book is not for people who want more customers, more sales ..and to make more money.

This book provides detailed instructions on how to use various marketing methods, including SEO, social media, and email marketing.

The tips and strategies in this book are proven to be effective, and have helped many businesses achieve success. If you're looking for a way to promote your business effectively and efficiently, this book is for you.

Are you tired of feeling like you're not doing enough to promote your business?

Are you tired of not seeing the results that you want?

Are you tired of not having enough time in the day to do everything?

Do you want more customers?

Do you want to see a difference in your business in the next 30 days?

Are you ready to see a difference in your business in the next 30 days?

If you're looking for ways to promote your business, our book can help.

This book covers the main foundations and aspects of marketing, from SEO to social media to email campaigns.

Implementing these tips will help you see a difference in your traffic and customer base in just 30 days!

Skeptics Read This: The methods mentioned in this book do work, and have been used by many businesses both small and large.

However, any marketing campaign will require effort and time in order to be successful. If you are not willing to put in the necessary work, then these methods may not be for you.

A skeptic would say that there is no guarantee that following the tips in this book will result in increased traffic and customers. They would also say that it is possible to implement these tips without spending any money, making this book's advice irrelevant.

If you are concerned why you have no website traffic, no customers & your website is not generating any sales - **the answer is your not marketing correctly**

- This book is still for you even if you have website traffic, as this will help you grow your business to the next level

How This Book Is Different

1. This book is different because it provides detailed instructions and step-by-step advice for implementing marketing strategies.

2. This book is different because it is international and has proven results from businesses around the world.

3. This book is different because it helps with SEO, social media marketing, email marketing, and outbound Marketing methods which will make a difference.

How To Read This Book

- I have a website and I just can't seem to get customers?

- What have you tried that has worked for your business?

- How do I use this book to solve my problems?

Read this book in the sections to help learn the methods and techniques to help grow your online business

My Story

This book is a great opportunity to help market your business using all methods of marketing. If you're starting a new website, existing website or e-commerce website, this book can help get traffic to your website and increase customers and sales.

These tips are proven to help international businesses, so implement them now and see a difference in the next 30 days.

I'm not asking you to believe in me, I'm asking you to believe in the advice and tips I'm providing.

These tips have been proven to help businesses of all sizes, so trust that they will work for you too. So there's really nothing to lose by trying these methods out.

If you want your business to be successful, you need to believe in yourself and have full confidence and clarity that you are on the right path.

The tips and advice I've provided in this book are sure to help promote your business, but if you're not confident in what you're doing, it will be difficult to succeed.

Stay positive, stay focused and stay determined, and your business will prosper.

- *Right opportunity?* What You Can Do to Promote Your Business at a Low Cost

- *Right person?* International Marketing Expert Ricky Whiting

- *Right time?* Now is the time to make these changes

"If not this, then what? If not you, then who? If not now, then when?"

The main topics that will be covered in the book.

Business Advice

Methods of marketing
- Different types of marketing you can introduce to your business
-

SEO
-How to use SEO to increase traffic to your website

Social Media
- Why use social media to promote your business

Methods of marketing

There are many different methods of marketing, and the best approach depends on the product or service being marketed, the target audience, and the budget.

Traditional methods such as television and print ads can be expensive, but they reach a wide audience.

More modern methods such as social media marketing and search engine optimisation can be more cost-effective, but they require a greater time commitment.

The most important thing is to identify the method or combination of methods that will work best for your business.

Only then can you start to see the results you want.

Research your target audience.

Before you can start promoting your business, you need to know who your target audience is.

This will help you determine the best way to reach them. Once you know who your target audience is, you can begin to create content that appeals to them.

Create a budget for your marketing efforts.

Once you have an idea of what methods you'll be using to promote your business, you need to create a budget.

This will help you stay on track and ensure that you're not spending more than you can afford. Keep in mind that some methods of marketing, such as search engine optimisation, can take time to see results. Others, such as social media marketing, can be very immediate.

Start promoting your business.
Now that you know what you're doing and how much you're willing to spend, it's time to start promoting your business.

There are a number of ways to do this, and the best approach depends on the method or methods you've chosen. If you're using social media, for example, you'll need to create content and post it regularly.

If you're using search engine optimisation, you'll need to make sure your website is optimised for the right keywords.

The most important thing is to be consistent with your efforts and track your results so you can see what's working and what isn't.

Evaluate your results.
After you've been promoting your business for a while, it's important to take a step back and evaluate your results.

This will help you determine what's working and what isn't so you can make adjustments as needed.

It will also help you see how far you've come and set goals for the future.

By following these tips, you can promote your business at a low cost and see the results you want.

Implement these strategies now to see a difference in the next 30 days.

SEO

Search Engine Optimisation, or "SEO" for short, is the practice of improving the ranking of a website on search engines.

The higher the ranking, the more likely people are to find the site. The main goal of SEO is to drive traffic to a website, but it can also be used to improve other aspects of a site, such as usability and conversion rates.

There are many benefits to investing in SEO, but the most important one is that it can help you reach your target audience.

With more and more people using search engines to find information online, it's essential that your website appears high in the results pages.

Otherwise, you're missing out on potential customers or clients. SEO can also lead to increased brand awareness and trust, as well as higher levels of customer satisfaction. In other words, investing in SEO is a smart business decision that can pay off in a number of ways.

To reach my target audience. It's essential to ensure that my website appears high in the search engine results pages or else I'm missing out on potential customers or clients.

SEO can also lead to increased brand awareness and trust, as well as higher levels of customer satisfaction. In other words, investing in SEO is a smart business decision that can pay off in a number of ways.

Social media marketing

Social media marketing is the process of using social media platforms to promote a product or service. It can be used to build brand awareness, generate leads, or increase sales.

There are a number of social media platforms that can be used for social media marketing, including Facebook, Twitter, LinkedIn, and Instagram.

When it comes to social media marketing, it's important to create content that is relevant and interesting to your target audience.

This will help you reach more people and encourage them to engage with your brand. It's also important to be consistent with your postings and interact with your followers on a regular basis. by doing this, you'll build relationships and trust, which can lead to increased sales.

Social media is a platform where people can interact with each other, share content, and connect with businesses. It's a powerful communications tool that can be used for marketing purposes.

There are many different social media platforms, such as Facebook, Twitter, Instagram, and Snapchat. Each one has its own unique features and audience.

When it comes to promoting your business on social media, it's important to choose the right platform. Not all platforms are created equal, and some may be more suitable for your business than others.

For example, if you're selling products or services to consumers, then Facebook would be a good choice. If you're targeting businesses, then LinkedIn would be a better option.

Social media networks

There are many social media networks that can be used for social media marketing, including Facebook, Twitter, LinkedIn, and Instagram.

When it comes to social media marketing, it's important to create content that is relevant and interesting to your target audience.

This will help you reach more people and encourage them to engage with your brand. It's also important to be consistent with your postings and interact with your followers on a regular basis. by doing this, you'll build relationships and trust, which can lead to increased sales.

Email marketing

Email marketing is the process of sending emails to potential or current customers with the goal of promoting a product or service.

It can be used to build relationships, generate leads, or increase sales. Email marketing is a very effective way to reach your target audience and can be done on a large or small scale.

When it comes to email marketing, it's important to create content that is relevant and interesting to your target audience. This will help you reach more people and encourage them to engage with your brand.

It's also important to be consistent with your postings and interact with your followers on a regular basis. by doing this, you'll build relationships and trust, which can lead to increased sales.

Outbound marketing

Outbound marketing is a type of marketing that focuses on getting the word out about a product or service through advertising, PR, and other forms of promotion.

It's often used as a way to increase brand awareness or generate leads. Outbound marketing can be very effective, but it can also be quite costly.

When it comes to outbound marketing, it's important to create content that is relevant and interesting to your target audience.

This will help you reach more people and encourage them to engage with your brand. It's also important to be consistent with your postings and interact with your followers on a regular basis.

by doing this, you'll build relationships and trust, which can lead to increased sales.

What is a business plan?

What is a business plan? In business, the term "business plan" refers to a written document that comprehensively outlines what your business is, where it is going, and how it will get there.

The business plan outlines in specific terms the financial objectives of your business, and how it will position itself to achieve those goals in the context of the current market landscape.

A well-crafted business plan should include:

1. An executive summary of your business.

2. A description of your products or services.

3. A market analysis, detailing your target market and competition.

4. A detailed description of your marketing and sales strategy.

5. A description of your company's management team and organisational structure.

6. Your company's financial projections, including income statements, balance sheets, and cash flow statements.

7. An appendix containing supporting documents, such as resumes, market research, and lease agreements.

What are the benefits of a business plan? A business plan is essential for any business, regardless of size.

It provides a roadmap for your business, and can help secure funding from investors or lenders.

But even if you don't need external financing, a business plan can still be a helpful tool to help you organise your thoughts and develop a clear strategy for growing your business.

Crafting an Effective Executive Summary:

The executive summary is the most important part of your business plan—it's where you make your pitch to potential investors, partners, and lenders.

The executive summary should be clear, concise, and compelling. It should give readers a snapshot of your business, and explain why you're confident that your business will be successful.

When crafting your executive summary, keep the following in mind:

1. Keep it short—no more than two pages.

2. Start with a brief overview of your business, including your company's mission statement and value proposition.

3. Describe your target market, and explain how you plan to reach them.

4. Give a brief overview of your products or services.

5. Discuss your sales and marketing strategy, including any unique selling points or competitive advantages you may have.

6. Summarise your financial projections, and explain how you plan to use any funding you're seeking.

7. Conclude with a brief statement of your long-term business goals.

Tips for Writing a Compelling Executive Summary:

Below is a provide structure to help you compose your executive summary:

1. Write it last–after you've completed the rest of your business plan. This will ensure that your executive summary is concise and focused.

2. Stick to the facts–avoid using hype or exaggerating your company's potential. investors are looking for a realistic assessment of your business.

3. Be clear and concise–use simple language that can be understood by anyone reading your business plan. Avoid jargon or industry-specific terminology.

4. Tell a story–use your executive summary to paint a picture of your business, and explain why you're passionate about it.

5. Focus on the future–investors are looking for businesses with potential for growth. Emphasise your company's long-term goals, and how you plan to achieve them.

2. Why do I need a business plan?

A business plan is important because it helps outline your business goals and strategies. Without a business plan, it can be difficult to stay on track and ensure that your business is heading in the right direction.

Having a business plan can also help you secure funding from investors or banks.

Creating a business plan doesn't have to be complicated. In fact, it can be as simple as answering a few questions about your business. Here are a few tips to get you started:

1. Define your business goals and objectives. What do you want to achieve with your business? What are your long-term and short-term goals?

Be specific and realistic in your goals so that you can easily measure your progress.

2. Outline your marketing strategies. How will you promote your business? Will you use online marketing, offline marketing, or a combination of both?

What methods will you use to reach your target audience? Again, be specific in your plans so that you can effectively track your results.

3. Describe your target market. Who are your potential customers? What needs do they have that your business can address? What are their buying habits?

The more you know about your target market, the better you can reach them with your marketing efforts.

4. Determine your pricing strategy. How will you price your products or services? Will you offer discounts or promotions?

Your pricing strategy should be based on your target market, competitors' prices, and the value of your product or service.

5. Create a sales and marketing budget. How much money do you need to promote your business?

How will you allocate your budget across different marketing channels? Knowing how much you're willing to spend on marketing will help you create a more effective and efficient plan.

6. Set a timeline for your goals. When do you want to achieve your business goals? Breaking down your goals into smaller, achievable milestones will help you stay on track and measure your progress.

7. Write down your action items. What specific tasks do you need to do to achieve your goals?

Who is responsible for each task? When will it be completed? Having a clear plan of action will help you execute your marketing strategies and achieve your desired results.

By following these tips, you can create a simple yet effective business plan that will help guide your marketing efforts.

Remember, your business plan should be flexible so that you can adjust it as needed as your business grows and changes.

3. How to create an effective business plan

Creating an effective business plan is essential to the success of any business.

The following steps will help you create a plan that will help your business achieve its goals.

1. Define your business goals. What do you want your business to achieve? Write down specific goals, such as increasing sales, expanding into new markets, or improving customer service.

2. Assess your current situation. What resources do you have available to you? What are your strengths and weaknesses?

3. Develop a strategy. How will you achieve your business goals? What tactics will you use?

4. Set a timeline for each goal. When do you want to achieve each goal?

5. Create a budget. How much money do you have to spend on marketing and promotion?

6. Implement your plan. Put your plan into action.

7. Monitor your progress. Regularly review your progress and make adjustments to your plan as needed.

By following these steps, you can develop an effective plan that will help you achieve your business goals. Remember to be flexible and adjust your plan as needed to ensure success.

4. What are the different types of plans, including financial and marketing plans?

There are different types of plans that business owners can use to help them succeed. The two most important plans are the financial plan and the marketing plan.

The financial plan is important because it helps business owners understand their current financial situation and make decisions about how to move forward.

The marketing plan is important because it helps business owners understand their target market and how to reach that market.

Both of these plans are important, and business owners should make sure they have both of them in place if they want to be successful.

5. What are the Key components of a successful marketing plan?

There are a few key components of a successful marketing plan. The first is to identify your target audience and what needs or desires they have that your product or service can fulfil.

Once you know who you're targeting, you need to create content that will appeal to them and drive them to your website. This content can be in the form of blog posts, articles, social media posts, email newsletters, or even videos.

Another important element of a successful marketing plan is SEO. You need to make sure your website is well-optimised for search engines so that you can rank higher and get more traffic.

Additionally, you should use other online channels such as social media and email marketing to drive traffic back to your website. And finally, you need to measure your results so that you can see what's working and what isn't.

By following these tips, you can create a low-cost marketing plan that will help you get more traffic and conversions.

Implement these strategies today and you'll see a difference in your business in the next 30 days.

6. Different ways to present your ideas in the best light possible, such as with infographics or videos

There are many different ways to present your ideas in the best light possible, such as with infographics or videos.

Infographics are a great way to present complex data in an easy-to-understand way, and they can be shared online easily.

Videos can also be a great way to present your ideas, and they can be shared online as well.

An infographic is a great way to present complex data in an easy-to-understand way. They can be shared online easily, and are a popular form of content.

According to the latest figures from YouTube, there are now over a billion users on the platform, and those users are watching over 6 billion hours of video a day.

As a business, it's important to understand these statistics, and to consider how you can use YouTube to reach your target audience.

Some interesting facts about YouTube include:

- 80% of all internet users visit YouTube
- Over 50% of adults in the US watch YouTube videos every day
- The average viewer watches around 5 hours of YouTube a week
- In 2017, YouTube generated $11.14 billion in ad revenue

As you can see, YouTube is a powerful platform with a huge reach. If you're not using YouTube to promote your business, you're missing out on a lot of potential customers.

There are a few things you need to keep in mind when creating YouTube videos for your business:

- Make sure the videos are high quality and interesting

- Optimise your videos for SEO by including keywords in the title and description

- Use annotations and calls to action to encourage viewers to visit your website or take other desired actions

- Create a channel trailer that gives viewers an overview of what they can expect from your channel

- Promote your videos on social media and other websites to drive traffic to them

If you follow these tips, you'll be able to create successful YouTube videos that promote your business and reach a wide audience.

YouTube isn't the only video platform out there, and it's not the only place where you can host your videos.

There are a number of other sites that offer video hosting services, and some of them may be a better fit for your needs.

Some popular video hosting platforms include:

- Vimeo
- Wistia
- Brightcove
- Kaltura

Each of these platforms has its own advantages and disadvantages, so it's important to do your research before choosing one.

You should also consider the cost of using each platform, as some of them charge monthly fees while others are free.

Once you've decided on a video hosting platform, you'll need to create your videos.

There are a few things you should keep in mind when creating your videos:

- Make sure the videos are high quality and interesting

- Optimise your videos for SEO by including keywords in the title and description

- Use annotations and calls to action to encourage viewers to visit your website or take other desired actions

- Promote your videos on social media and other websites to drive traffic to them

If you follow these tips, you'll be able to create successful videos that promote your business and reach a wide audience.

In addition to using YouTube and other video hosting platforms to promote your business, you can also use social media sites like Facebook, Twitter, and Instagram.

These sites have billions of users, and they offer businesses a great way to reach a large audience.

When promoting your business on social media, it's important to:

- Use images and videos to get attention

- Post interesting and engaging content

- Use calls to action to encourage people to visit your website or take other desired actions

- Promote your posts on other websites and in email newsletters

If you follow these tips, you'll be able to reach a large audience with your social media promotion.

7. Tips for building your credibility online, like by using social media accounts and adding testimonials on your website

One great way to build your credibility online is by using social media accounts.

For example, if you have a Facebook page for your business, make sure to add a link to your website on your profile and post interesting content that will engage your followers.

You can also use social media platforms like Twitter and Instagram to share photos and videos of your products or services.

Another way to boost your credibility is by adding testimonials on your website. Make sure to include quotes from happy customers who have had a positive experience with your business. This will help persuade potential customers to give you a chance.

Testimonials are a great way to show potential customers that you're a credible business.

By including quotes from happy customers on your website, you can show them that you're worth giving a chance. Plus, positive testimonials can help persuade other customers to give your business a try.

If you want to get more exposure for your business, consider guest blogging on other websites.

This is a great way to reach a new audience and showcase your expertise.

When writing your guest blog post, make sure to include a link back to your website so that readers can learn more about your business.

Finally, another low-cost way to promote your business is by using search engine optimisation (SEO).

This involves optimising your website so that it appears as the top result when people search for relevant keywords. By ranking high in search engines, you'll get more traffic to your website and increase your chances of making a sale.

Implementing these low-cost marketing strategies will help you boost your credibility online and attract more customers.

8. How to get feedback from others about your idea before you invest too much time and money into it?

One way to get feedback about your business idea before investing too much time and money is to ask friends and family for their opinion.

Additionally, you can reach out to online forums or social media groups that are related to your industry. By doing this, you'll get a sense of whether or not there is interest in your product or service, and you can also gather valuable feedback from potential customers.

Feedback is important for a business owner because it allows them to gauge how well their product or service is being received by the public.

Additionally, feedback can help business owners identify areas where they may need to make changes or improvements to their product or service. Feedback is also valuable because it can help business owners understand what potential customers want and need.

When it comes to negative feedback, business owners need to take a few key steps. First, they should never ignore negative feedback.

By ignoring it, you're essentially telling customers that their opinion doesn't matter. Additionally, negative feedback can provide valuable insights into what needs to be changed or improved with your product or service.

Second, business owners should always respond to negative feedback in a respectful and professional manner.

Thank the customer for taking the time to provide their feedback and then try to address their concerns. It's also important to apologise for any inconvenience or problems that may have occurred.

Finally, business owners should always try to learn from any mistakes made in the past. By taking these steps, they can avoid making the same mistakes in the future and provide a better experience for their customers.

Third, business owners should take advantage of social media platforms to interact with potential and current customers.

Social media platforms like Facebook, Twitter, and Instagram offer businesses a great way to connect with their target audience. Additionally, social media platforms can be used to build relationships with customers, which can lead to increased sales and customer loyalty.

Finally, business owners should always remember that promoting their business doesn't have to be expensive.

There are a number of low-cost or even free marketing techniques that can be just as effective as more traditional methods.

For example, businesses can use word-of-mouth marketing or online reviews to reach new customers.

Additionally, businesses can take advantage of social media platforms to connect with potential and current customers.

By using these low-cost or free marketing techniques, businesses can save money while still promoting their business effectively.

*** Bonus Email Template ***

Dear (customer name),

I'm so glad you enjoyed your experience with our company! It means a lot to us that you had a good time and would recommend us to others.

We really appreciate your online review, and I wanted to make sure you know how much we appreciate it.

Thank you for your kind words, and we hope you'll visit us again soon!

Sincerely,
(Your name)

9. The importance of making a good first impression, no matter what type of business you have.

When you're starting a business, it's important to make a good first impression.

This means putting your best foot forward and making sure that your website and marketing materials are professional and polished. It also means being active on social media and networking with other businesses.

Your website and marketing materials are the first impression that customers will have of your business.

If they're not professional and polished, customers will assume that your business is also unprofessional.

It's also important to be active on social media and networking with other businesses. This will help you build relationships and referrals.

"Your first impression is your last impression,"

says real estate mogul and TV personality Ryan Serhant.

This is especially true when it comes to your website and marketing materials. If they're not professional and polished, customers will assume that your business is also unprofessional. It's important to put your best foot forward and make a good first impression.

It can make the difference between being seen or ignored. If you are dressed nicely and take proper care of your appearance, the customer will assume that you take the same care with their order.

Here is one instance: If a customer sees an employee answering phones while wearing sweatpants and a t-shirt they might think, "Why would this establishment spend any money on marketing or advertising if they don't invest in their employees?" Or even worse, "What if my food was prepared by someone like them? My health could be at risk!"

One way to avoid this is to dress according to the program for your shift.

Be sure not do wear anything so formal that it interferes with tasks at hand though! For example, an apron or company polo shirt is usually a good idea.

When it comes to your website, first impressions are key. Make sure that your website is up-to-date and reflects the current state of your business.

If you have an online store, ensure that your products are well-represented and that customers can easily check out.

If you're providing a service, make sure that your pricing is clear and that potential customers can easily contact you to book an appointment.

Your website should also be mobile-friendly, as more and more people are using their phones to browse the internet.

If your website isn't mobile-friendly, you could be losing out on potential customers.

If you're not sure how to create a professional website, there are many services that can help, such as WordPress or WooCommerce. You can also hire a web designer to create a custom website for you.

In addition to having a professional website, it's also important to be active on social media. Social media is a great way to connect with potential and current customers, build relationships, and generate referrals.

Make sure to post regularly and interact with other users. If you're not sure how to get started, there are many guides and resources available online.

Finally, networking with other businesses is a great way to promote your business. Attend local events and meetups, join Chamber of Commerce or business groups, or volunteer for local causes.

This is a great way to meet potential customers and build relationships with other businesses.

When you're starting a business, it's important to make a good first impression.

This means putting your best foot forward and making sure that your website and marketing materials are professional and polished.

It also means being active on social media and networking with other businesses.

These activities will help you build relationships and generate referrals. Implement these tips and strategies now to see a difference in the next 30 days.

10. How to stand out from the competition by offering unique products or services

Your business can stand out from the competition by offering unique products or services.

When you offer something that is different from what your competitors are offering, you can attract new customers who are looking for something new.

Additionally, you can also focus on developing a strong branding strategy that helps your business stand out from the rest.

By creating a distinct identity for your company, you can make it easier for potential customers to remember you and what you offer.

If you're looking for niche products to start selling, here are a few ideas:

-Unique jewellery designs
-Handcrafted furniture
-Customised clothing
-Artisanal food products

If you want to focus on branding, here are a few tips:

-Develop a strong visual identity for your business. This can include creating a logo, choosing a colour palette, and developing other visual elements that will be associated with your company.

-Make sure your branding is consistent across all of your marketing materials, including your website, social media accounts, and print collateral.

-Tell customers why they should choose your business. What makes you different from your competitors? Why should someone do business with you instead of someone else? Be clear about what sets you apart and make sure this message comes through in all of your marketing communications.

And so, by offering unique products or services and/or developing a strong branding strategy, you can make it easier for potential customers to remember you and what you have to offer.

This can help to set you apart from the competition, and may encourage more people to do business with you.

11. The best ways to market your business on a tight budget

There are many ways to market your business on a tight budget. The following are some of the best methods:

1. SEO: Optimising your website for search engines can be a cost-effective way to drive traffic to your site. There are many free or low-cost tools and services available to help you optimise your site.

2. Social Media: Marketing your business on social media platforms can be a low-cost way to reach a large audience. There are many free or low-cost tools and services available to help you create and manage social media accounts.

3. Email Marketing: Sending out regular email newsletters can be a cost-effective way to reach current and potential customers. There are many free or low-cost email

marketing services available.

4. Outbound Marketing: Traditional outbound marketing techniques, such as direct mail and print advertising, can be costly. However, there are ways to minimise the cost of these methods by targeting your audience more efficiently.

There are many other low-cost marketing ideas not mentioned here. The important thing is to get started and experiment with different marketing techniques to see what works best for your business.

Implementing even a few of these ideas can make a big difference in the success of your business.

12. Tips for generating leads and converting them into paying customers

1. When it comes to generating leads, quality is always better than quantity. Make sure that your website and content are of the highest quality so that you can attract more qualified leads.

2. Use lead capture forms on your website so that you can collect information from potential customers. This will help you follow-up with them and convert them into paying customers.

3. Use social media to reach out to potential customers and followers. Make sure to post valuable content that will interest them, and use effective call-to-action buttons to encourage them to take action.

4. Email marketing is still a very effective way to reach out to potential customers.

Make sure to design beautiful emails that will stand out in their inbox, and use effective subject lines to encourage them to open your email.

5. Outbound marketing techniques like cold calling and direct mail can still be effective if done correctly. Make sure to target your audience properly and craft a compelling message that will interest them.

By following these tips, you can promote your business at a low cost and generate more leads and customers. Implement these strategies today to see a difference in your business in the next 30 days

13. How to create a sales funnel that will turn prospects into lifelong fans

A sales funnel is a process that takes potential customers from the point of awareness of your product or service to the point of purchase.

It typically involves several steps, such as creating a strong offer, driving targeted traffic to your offer, converting leads into customers, and providing excellent customer service.

By using a sales funnel, you can turn prospects into lifelong fans of your business.

A well-constructed sales funnel can help turn prospects into lifelong fans of your business. Here are a few tips for creating a sales funnel that will work for you:

1. Start by creating a strong offer that is irresistible to your target audience. This

could be a free trial, a discount, or something else that is attractive to your audience.

2. Drive targeted traffic to your offer using SEO, social media, email marketing, or other methods.

3. Convert prospects into leads by getting them to take action on your offer.

4. Nurture your leads and build relationships with them so they become customers.

5. Offer excellent customer service so your customers remain loyal to your business.

6. Continuously test and improve your sales funnel so it is always performing at its best.

By following these tips, you can create a sales funnel that will help you increase sales and grow your business.

Low-cost promotion is possible if you know how to market your business effectively. Use the tips above to get started promoting your business today!

14. Strategies for upselling and cross-selling to boost your revenue

There are a few key strategies that you can use to boost your revenue through upselling and cross-selling.

When upselling, try to focus on products that are complementary to the ones that the customer is already interested in.

This will make it more likely that they will be persuaded to make the purchase.

Another key strategy is cross-selling. This involves selling additional products to customers that they may be interested in.

For example, if you sell clothes, you could also sell accessories such as belts and scarves.

If you are running an e-commerce website, you can cross-sell products by including links to complementary products on the product pages.

You can also highlight related products on the home page and on other pages of the website.

Upselling is an easy way to boost profits because it encourages customers to buy more expensive items.

It also builds customer loyalty, as customers are more likely to return if they are happy with their previous purchase.

Another reason upselling is successful is because it allows businesses to sell more products at a higher margin.

This means that businesses can make more money from each sale, which can help to boost profits.

15. Ways to use content marketing to drive traffic to your website

This is a book that provides tips and strategies for using content marketing to drive traffic to your website.

It covers all aspects of content marketing, from SEO to social media networks to email campaigns.

The advice in the book is proven and has helped businesses from around the world increase their customer base and sales.

If you're looking for ways to improve your website's traffic, this book can help get you started.

** Bonus 10 Top tips for e-commerce websites ***

1. Make sure your website is optimised for search engines.

If you want your e-commerce website to be successful, it's important to make sure that it is optimised for search engines.

This means making sure that the site is coded in a way that makes it easy for Google and other search engines to index and rank.

You also need to include keywords throughout your site content so that potential customers can easily find you online.

2. Produce high-quality content that is relevant to your target audience.

If you want your website to be successful, it's important to produce high-quality content that is relevant to your target audience.

This means creating content that is useful and engaging for visitors, and that speaks directly to the needs of your customers.

By producing great content, you'll not only attract more visitors but also keep them coming back for more.

3. Use social media to promote your content and attract new customers.

To promote your content and attract new customers, you can use social media networks such as Facebook, Twitter, and LinkedIn.

These platforms provide a great way to reach a large audience with your content, and they also allow you to connect with potential customers on a more personal level.

4. Email marketing is still an effective way to reach your target audience.

Yes, email marketing is still an effective way to reach your target audience.

Mailchimp is a great tool for creating and sending email newsletters, and it provides you with a range of templates and tools to make the process easy.

By sending regular email newsletters to your customers, you can keep them up-to-date with your latest products and services, and you can also encourage them to visit your website.

5. Use paid advertising to reach more people quickly and easily.

One example of paid advertising is Google Ads. With Google Ads, you can create text or display ads that will appear on the Google search results page and other websites across the web.

This allows you to reach a large number of potential customers quickly and easily, and it also allows you to target your ads to specific audiences.

6. Create a strong branding strategy to help differentiate your business from the competition.

Branding is important because it helps customers recognise and remember your business. By creating a strong branding strategy, you can help your business stand out from the competition and make it easier for customers to find and remember you.

Branding also helps to create a sense of trust between your customers and your business, which can encourage them to buy from you.

7. Use web analytics to track your website's traffic and performance.

Google Analytics is a free tool that allows you to track the traffic and performance of your website. It provides detailed information about who is visiting your site, how they are finding it, and what they are doing once they get there.

This information can be used to help improve the overall effectiveness of your website and increase its traffic and sales.

8. Keep your website updated with the latest news and offers.

Offers and promotions can be a great way to increase sales, but it's important to make sure that they are well-targeted and effective.

To ensure that your offers are effective, you need to make sure that they are relevant to your target audience, and that you offer something of value in return.

You also need to make sure that your website is easy to navigate and that the checkout process is smooth and user-friendly.

9. Invest in online marketing tools and techniques to help improve your results.

Here a 5 tools which will help grow your business.

1. Google Analytics
2. MailChimp
3. Google Ads
4. Facebook Insights
5. Twitter Analytics

10. Always be prepared to adjust your marketing strategy

IMPORTANT TIP! No matter how effective your marketing strategy is, you'll always need to be prepared to adjust it in order to keep up with the competition.

By being flexible and adaptable, you'll be able to react quickly to changes in the market and ensure that your business remains competitive.

16. The most effective methods for getting found online, including SEO and PPC campaigns

There are a variety of effective methods for getting found online, including SEO and PPC campaigns.

SEO, or search engine optimisation, is the process of improving the visibility and ranking of a website or web page in search engine results pages. PPC, or pay-per-click, is a type of online advertising where advertisers pay a publisher (typically a search engine, social media site, or email service) each time their ad is clicked.

By using both SEO and PPC together, businesses can greatly improve their chances of being found by potential customers online.

3 easy hacks for SEO

1. Use keywords in your website's title and throughout the content to help improve your ranking in search engine results pages (SERPs).

2. Make sure your website is easy to navigate, with clear titles for each page and a user-friendly design.

3. Regularly update your website's content with fresh, relevant information to keep visitors coming back.

3 easy hacks for PPC

1. Always bid on keywords that are relevant to your business and have high commercial intent.

2. Make sure your ads are well-written and engaging, and that they target the right audience.

3. Use negative keywords to prevent your ads from appearing alongside irrelevant search results.

Thank You!

Thank you for reading! I hope this information was helpful and that you will be able to use these tips to promote your business.

If you would like to learn more about how to promote your business, please connect with me on Instagram @rickywhiting for more information.

I would be happy to help!

Printed in Great Britain
by Amazon

37201192R00056